THE LOVE OF CATS

THE LOVE OF CATS

The Daily Telegraph

Anthology of Cats

CELIA HADDON

HEADLINE

First published in 1992
by HEADLINE BOOK PUBLISHING PLC

10 9 8 7 6 5 4 3 2 1

British Library Cataloguing in Publication Data

Haddon, Celia
    Love of Cats: "Daily Telegraph" Anthology of Cats
    I. Title
    808 . 8036

    ISBN 0-7472-0615-5

Design and computer page make up by Penny Mills

Illustration reproduction by Koford International, Singapore

Printed and bound in Great Britain by Butler and Tanner Limited, Frome

HEADLINE BOOK PUBLISHING PLC
Headline House
79 Great Titchfield Street
London W1P 7FN

To Kate and Jack and Mungo and Sampson

Author's Note

Please help homeless, neglected or ill-treated cats and kittens by
supporting cat rescue homes and charities like
the Cats Protection League and the
Feline Advisory Bureau.

CONTENTS

CATS AND THEIR HUMAN PETS

The love of humans for cats is as strong as the love of humans for other humans. Sometimes stronger. For, despite the gulf between our species, it is a relationship of two equal personalities – if one assumes that human beings are equal to cats, that is. Not all cats do. Some of them make it clear that in their eyes humans are simply charming household pets.

Not for cats the loving dependence and self-abnegation of dogs. They retain the right at all times to lead their own lives and to look after their own interests. Many of them adopt an air of affectionate superiority towards their humans.

Some people persist in disliking them for this independence of spirit. Man has chosen to dominate animals rather than accept and understand them, seeing them as subjects for his rule rather than beings for his friendship. He has thus often preferred the self-abandonment of the dog to the detachment of the cat.

Devotion, loyalty and self sacrifice are not absent from the cat-human relationship, being found frequently on the human side. Let us then celebrate men like Philibert Commerson, the eighteenth-century French explorer. While he was sailing off the coast of Patagonia, the natives rowed out in canoes and offered him a dazzlingly beautiful young girl in

exchange for the scruffy ship's cat. The noble Frenchman refused to betray his animal companion.

Some cat lovers turn over their homes to the greater convenience of felines. Henry Hastings, a seventeenth-century squire, had a home in which 'the great chairs had litters of young cats in them which were not to be disturbed, he having always three or four attending him at dinner'. In order to be fed, himself, he had 'a little white round stick of fourteen inches long lying by his trencher, that he might defend such meat as he had no mind to part with to them'.

Two centuries later in Italy at Naples, Monsignore Capecelatro, a retired bishop, ran his household for the benefit of his Angora cats, all with romantic names like Pantalone, Desdemona, Otello. His chaplains served the cats at table. An English visitor reported: 'On the bishop requesting one of the chaplains to help the Signora Desdemona,' (one of the cats) 'the butler stepped up to his lordship and observed, "My lord, La Signora Desdemona will prefer waiting for the roasts."'

Cats seem to have a sixth sense about taking up residence with their admirers. First one cat, then another, then a few visiting cats… some people end up with an awful lot of cats.

When an American professor went to tea with the writer Thomas Hardy in 1900 he was amazed to find scores of cats being fed. He asked if all of them were the writer's cats. 'Oh dear, no,' was the reply. 'Some of them are, and some are cats who come regularly to have tea, and some are still other cats, not invited by us, but who seem to find about this time of day that tea will be going.' Wise cats know exactly when to drop by.

The sixteenth-century essayist Michel Montaigne perceived the great truth that we do not rule the animal kingdom. The natural world has its own ways, of which we know only a little. And this insight, which a modern ecologist would applaud, was partly thanks to his cat.

Of all creatures man is the most miserable and frail, and therewithall the proudest and disdainfullest... How knoweth he by the virtue of his understanding the inward and secret motions of beasts? By what comparison from them to us doth he conclude the brutishness he ascribeth unto them? When I am playing with my cat, who knows whether she have more sport in dallying with me than I have in gaming with her? We entertain one another with mutual apish tricks. If I have my hour to begin or to refuse, so hath she hers... The defect which hindreth the communication between them and us, why may it not as well be in us as in them? It is a matter of divination to guess in whom the fault is that we understand not one another. For we understand them no more than they us. By the same reason, may they as well esteem us beasts as we them.

Cat lovers, I am pleased to say, do not let the sneers of the world interfere with their devotional duties. Christmas, in particular, seems to bring out their loving feelings. Cats receive presents, are given special Christmas dinners and almost always take part in unwrapping gifts under the tree. Some cat lovers go even further. A friend gave the religious writer Evelyn Underhill a special cat crib. This probably had (the letter referring to it is not clear) cats as well as ox and ass adoring the Christ child. And in the magazine, *Notes and Queries*, for 31 December 1938, a reader under the pseudonym of Ignoto wrote about the cat lover who gave her cats a special Christmas tree.

I read somewhere – in Lord Broughton's Memoirs, I think – of an old lady who prepared a Christmas tree for her cats. It was hung with herrings and they walked round it solemnly before being presented with the special delights it supplied. They must have been well trained not to spring up and detach the fish.

John Rich was the manager of Covent Garden in the eighteenth century and is perhaps best known as 'the father of pantomime'. He was devoted to cats and kept many of them. In 1739 a young actress later to become a great star, Peg Woffington, came to London looking for a job. She argued her way into his office and this is what she found.

The great manager... was lolling in ungraceful ease on a sofa, holding a play in one hand, and in the other a teacup, from which he sipped frequently. Around him were seven and twenty cats of all sizes, colours and kinds. Toms and tabbies, old cats and kittens, tortoiseshells, Maltese, brindles, white, black and yellow cats of every description. Some were frisking over the floor, others asleep on the rug; one was licking the buttered toast on his breakfast plate, another was engaged in drinking the cream for his tea, two cats lay on his knee, one was asleep on his shoulder, and another sat demurely on his head. Peg Woffington was astounded at the sight. Rich to her mind had for many years been the greatest man in the world. The menagerie of grimalkins, amid which he lay so carelessly, was so different an environment from her conception of the study of the Covent Garden theatre manager, that she was embarrassed into silence.

To a Cat

Stately, kindly, lordly friend,
    Condescend
Here to sit by me, and turn
Glorious eyes that smile and burn,
Golden eyes, love's lustrous meed,
On the golden page I read.

All your wondrous wealth of hair
    Dark and fair,
Silken-shaggy, soft and bright
As the clouds and beams of night,
Pays my reverent hand's caress
Back with friendlier gentleness.

Dogs may fawn on all and some
    As they come;
You, a friend of loftier mind,
Answer friends alone in kind.
Just your foot upon my hand
Softly bids it understand.

Wild on woodland ways your sires
   Flashed like fires:
Fair as flame and fierce and fleet
As with wings on wingless feet
Shone and sprang your mother, free,
Bright and brave as wind or sea.

Free and proud and glad as they,
   Here today
Rests or roams their radiant child,
Vanquished not, but reconciled,
Free from curb of aught above
Save the lovely curb of love.

              ALGERNON SWINBURNE

The nineteenth-century French philosopher Hippolyte Taine was passionate about cats. The full extent of his feelings came to light after his death. Twelve love sonnets, the only poems he wrote, were discovered. They were dedicated to Puss, Ebene and Mitonne 'by their friend, master and servant'. Here is one of them, titled *Happiness*, in translation.

Wisdom dwells, O venerable cat,
In your untroubled heart and rounded eyes:
Comfortable by the fireside your ceaseless purring
Is the outward echo of harmonious dreams.

To sleep the sleep of the Gods,
You curl youself into a ball, O predestined soul;
Leaving care and worry to that damned race
Who till the soil and probe the mysteries of the heavens.

As detached from the world's woes as a
    Brahmin,
You lap happiness from that deep cup,
From which mankind sips only
    malady and death.

A tragic mirage of Eden lost
Appears, as in a magic mirror,
In the limpid tranquillity of your
    golden eyes.

Stories of cats and clerics seem to abound in cat history. Robert Stephen Hawker, the Victorian vicar of the small parish in Cornwall and a poet known for the ballad, *And Shall Trelawney Die?*, took his cats to church with him. (There was even a rumour that he had excommunicated one of them for killing a mouse on a Sunday.) He was in the habit of petting them while saying prayers. His son-in-law reports:

In his love of birds and beasts Hawker was like St Francis of Assisi... He always kept a number of dogs and cats, which occasionally accompanied him to church. 'In Mr Hawker's judgement,' says a writer in the *Standard*, 'all the creatures had a certain right of admission to God's house. He sometimes appeared at his lectern attended by four or five cats, unusual but graceful acolytes, who, as he assured us, allowing for an occasional display of youthful vivacity, rarely conducted themselves otherwise than with great propriety.'

At one time he had nine cats. 'In the evening,' writes a friend, 'he led them to the cat-house. They had all names. Each waited till he pronounced its name, and then jumped up to the shelf on which they reposed. His dog, Dustyfoot, also went to church, and, like the dog in "Woodstock", generally behaved very well there. But once, when Mr Hawker went into the pulpit, it followed him up the steps, and remained by his side to the end of the discourse...' One of his cats he called his most righteous cat, because whenever he missed it, he generally found it waiting at the church door.

The Kitten and the Falling Leaves

That way look, my Infant, lo!
What a pretty baby-show!
See the kitten on the wall,
Sporting with the leaves that fall,
Withered leaves – one – two – and three –
From the lofty elder tree!…
But the kitten, how she starts,
Crouches, stretches, paws and darts!
First at one, and then its fellow,
Just as light, and just as yellow…

What intenseness of desire
In her upward eye of fire!
With a tiger-leap half-way,
Now she meets the coming prey,
Lets it go as fast, and then
Has it in her power again…
Such a light of gladness breaks,
Pretty kitten! from thy freaks, –
Spreads with such a living grace
O'er my little Dora's face;
Yes, the sight so stirs and charms
Thee, Baby, laughing in my arms,
That almost I could repine
That your transports are not mine…
Now and then I may possess
Hours of perfect gladsomeness,
–Pleased by any random toy;
By a kitten's busy joy,
Or an infant's laughing eye
Sharing in the ecstasy;
I would fare like that or this,
Find my wisdom in my bliss;
Keep the sprightly soul awake,
And have faculties to take,
Even from things by sorrow wrought,
Matter for a jocund thought,
Spite of care, and spite of grief,
To gambol with Life's falling leaf.

WILLIAM WORDSWORTH

Edward Lear is an exemplar for all cat lovers to copy. He lived in the South of France with his cat, Foss. Henry Strachey recorded the extent of his devotion to Foss.

When staying at Cannes at Christmas 1882, I was invited by Mr Lear to go over to San Remo to spend a few days with him. Mr Lear's villa was large, and the second he had built: the first became unbearable to him from a large hotel having been planted in front of it. So he put his new house in a place by the sea, where, as he said, nothing could interrupt his light unless the fishes built. The second house was exactly like the first. This, Mr Lear explained to me, was necessary, or else Foss, his cat, might not have approved of the new villa. At breakfast the morning after I arrived, this much-thought-of, though semi-tailed, cat jumped in at the window and ate a piece of toast from my hand. This, I found, was considered an event; when visitors stayed at Villa Tennyson, Foss generally hid himself in the back regions; but his recognition of me was a sort of 'guinea stamp', which seemed to please Mr Lear greatly, and assure him of my fitness to receive the constant acts of kindness he was showing me.

For some of us, cats are an inspiration. Florence Nightingale, that tough Victorian lady who campaigned all her life for proper nursing and better drains, showed a great tenderness for her many Persian cats. Her letters to friends reported their liaisons and made plans for homing their kittens – 'a matter as weighty as a Royal succession'. Here are some of her thoughts on cats.

Poor Mrs Herbert told me that her chief comfort was in a little Chinese dog of his [her dead husband's]... which used to come and kiss her eyelids and lick the tears from her cheeks. I remember thinking this childish. But now I don't. My cat does just the same to me. Dumb beasts observe you so much more than talking beings; and know so much better what you are thinking of...

I learn the lesson of life from a little kitten of mine, one of two. The old cat comes in and says, very cross, 'I didn't ask you in here, I like to have my Missis to myself!' And he runs at them. The bigger and handsomer kitten runs away, but the littler one *stands her ground* and when the old enemy comes near enough kisses his nose, and makes the peace. That is the lesson of life, to kiss one's enemy's nose, always standing one's ground...

I must strive to see only God in my friends, and God in my cats.

There are also times for some of us when cats are what makes life worth living. Christopher Smart, a poet of the eighteenth century, was put in an asylum when he started literally 'to pray without ceasing'. There he wrote a long religious poem titled *Jubilate Deo*, which has some wonderful and weird lines about his cat, Jeoffry. Lunatic asylums were grim places and Jeoffry must have been a comfort to the poor poet.

For I will consider my Cat Jeoffry.
For he is the servant of the Living God, duly and daily serving him.
For at the first glance of the glory of God in the East he worships in his
    way.
For is this done by wreathing his body seven times round with elegant
    quickness.
For then he leaps up to catch the musk, which is the blessing of God upon
    his prayer.
For he rolls upon prank to work it in.
For having done duty and received blessing he begins to consider himself.
For this he performs in ten degrees.
For first he looks upon his forepaws to see if they are clean.
For secondly he kicks up behind to clear away there.
For thirdly he works it upon stretch with the forepaws extended.
For fourthly he sharpens his paws by wood.
For fifthly he washes himself.
For sixthly he rolls upon wash.
For seventhly he fleas himself, that he may not be interrupted upon
    the beat.
For eighthly he rubs himself against a post.
For ninthly he looks up for his instructions.
For tenthly he goes in quest of food.
For having considered God and himself he will consider his neighbour.
For if he meets another cat he will kiss her in kindness.
For when he takes his prey he plays with it to give it a chance.

For one mouse in seven escapes by his dallying.

For when his day's work is done his business more properly begins.

For he keeps the Lord's watch in the night against the adversary.

For he counteracts the powers of darkness by his electrical skin and glaring eyes.

For he counteracts the Devil, who is death, by brisking about the life.

For in his morning orisons he loves the sun and the sun loves him.

For he is of the tribe of Tiger.

For the Cherub Cat is a term of the Angel Tiger.

For he has the subtlety and hissing of a serpent, which in goodness he suppresses.

For he will not do destruction, if he is well-fed, neither will he spit without provocation.

For he purrs in thankfulness, when God tells him he's a good Cat.

And he is an instrument for the children to learn benevolence upon.

For every house is incomplete without him and a blessing is lacking in the spirit.

A GLAD CHRISTMASTIDE FOR YOU

CATS IN THE NURSERY

From our earliest years cats become part of our lives. Even if we do not live with a cat in the family, moggies reign supreme in nursery literature. Cats are the wise and resourceful heroes of fairy tales like Dick Whittington and Puss in Boots: they appear in animal tales; and they are the subject of many nursery rhymes.

One of the earliest literary cats appears in a collection of stories about a cunning fox called Reynard. Written about eight centuries ago and subsequently appearing in several different versions, this 'beast epic' includes a cat called Tybert. So popular was it, that English cats are still called Tibby or Tibbles after Tybert and stories from it still find their way into the modern nursery.

Cats help educate us at an early age. In alphabet books, C almost always stands for Cat. And, before the vagaries of educational fashion, 'The Cat Sat On The Mat' was one of the first sentences taught in children's reading books.

In nursery rhymes, cats heavily outnumber dogs. 'This is probably because cats have been inside the house rather longer than dogs,' says Nicholas Tucker, a lecturer in psychology at Sussex University who has made a special study of animals in children's literature. 'The dog is a guardian outside the house. It is Daddy's animal, while the cat is Mummy's.'

Some of these rhymes, like 'Ding, dong, bell, pussy's in the well', hark back to the cruel days when it was fair game for human beings to torture cats for fun. In the eighteenth century rhymes like this worried nursery reformers, so writers for children like Ann and Jane Taylor published verses exhorting their young readers instead to be kind to cats.

'The people who were advocating children's literature were also those who had a feeling for the proper treatment of animals,' maintains Nicholas Tucker. 'They wanted children to grow up to be good people and they believed that if children treated animals badly when they were young, they would grow up to treat human beings badly.'

Cats slink into nonsense rhymes too. Edward Lear, who wrote nonsense rhymes for children, was a passionate feliphile, so cats naturally appeared in his rhymes and his pictures. It is to him we owe the story of the Owl and the Pussy Cat, one of the best-loved verses of childhood.

Perhaps the nicest things about nursery cats is that almost everybody knows them. Lord Ernle was once invited to dinner by Queen Victoria and asked his little daughter if she had a message for the queen. 'Oh yes,' she said, 'ask her to give me the little mouse that lives under the chair.'

After dinner, Lord Ernle delivered the message and Queen Victoria (for once) was very amused. She called up several of the other guests and retold the story. But one elderly peer didn't see the point of the story. The Queen turned on him indignantly and said, 'What, Lord —, don't you know "Pussy cat, pussy cat, where have you been?"'

Dick Whittington.

Here is the Scottish version of the nursery rhyme known and loved by Queen Victoria. The word 'baudrons' is the Scottish word for 'cat'.

Poussie, poussie, baudrons,
Where hae ye been?
I've been at London
To see the queen!

Poussie, poussie, baudrons,
What got ye there?
I got a guid fat mousikie
Rinnin' up a stair!

Poussie, poussie, baudrons,
What did ye do wi't?
I put it in my meal-pock,
To eat it to my bread!

Not all nursery cats are sympathetic characters. The cats that appear in *Struwwelpeter, or Merry Stories and Funny Pictures* by Heinrich Hoffman, translated into English in 1860, are odious told-you-sos.

It almost makes me cry to tell
What foolish Harriet befell.
Mamma and Nurse went out one day,
And left her all alone to play;
Now on the table close at hand
A box of matches chanced to stand;
And kind Mamma and Nurse had told her
That, if she touched them, they should scold her.
But Harriet said, 'Oh what a pity!
For when they burn it is so pretty;
They crackle so, and spit and flame;
Mamma, too, often does the same.'
     The pussy-cats heard this,
     And they began to hiss
     And stretch their claws and raise their paws,
     'Me-ow!' they said, 'Me-ow, me-o,
     You'll burn to death if you do so.'

But Harriet would not take advice,
She lit a match, it was so nice;
It crackled so, it burned so clear,
Exactly like the picture here.
She jumped for joy, and ran about
And was too pleased to put it out.

The pussy-cats saw this
And said, 'Oh naughty, naughty Miss!'
And stretched their claws and raised their paws,
'This is very, very wrong, you know!
Me-ow, me-o, me-ow, me-o,
·You will be burned if you do so.'

And so! Oh! what a dreadful thing!
The fire has caught her apron string;
Her apron burns, her arms, her hair,
She burns all over everywhere.
     Then how the pussy-cats did mew,
     What else, poor pussies, could they do?
     They screamed for help, 'twas all in vain!
     So then they said, 'We'll scream again;
     Make haste, make haste, me-ow, me-o
     She'll burn to death, we told her so.'

So she was burnt with all her clothes,
And arms, and hair, and eyes, and nose,
Till she had nothing more to lose
Except her little scarlet shoes;
And nothing else but these was found
Among her ashes on the ground.
     And when the good cats sat beside
     The smoking ashes, how they cried!
     'Me-ow, me-oo, me-ow, me-oo,
     What will Mamma and Nursey do?'
     Their tears ran down their cheeks so fast
     They made a little pond at last.

[29]

Two More Scottish Nursery Rhymes

Pussie at the fireside
Suppin' up brose,
Doon came a cinder
And burnt pussy's nose.
Och, said pussy,
That's no fair.
Weel, said the cinder,
Ye shouldna been there.

There was a wee bit mousikie,
That lived in Gilberaty-O,
It couldno' get a bite o' cheese,
For cheatie pussy-catty-O.

It said unto the cheeseky,
'Oh fain would I be at ye-O,
If 'twere no' for the cruel claws
Of cheatie pussy-catty-O.'

The nursery rhyme cat who fiddled while the dog jumped over the moon is one of many musical felines. Medieval carvings in churches often show a cat playing the fiddle or bagpipes. In these two rhymes, the 'crowdy' is a word for the 'crwth', an early version of the fiddle.

A cat came fiddling out of a barn
With a pair of bagpipes under her arm;
She could sing nothing but 'fiddle-cum-fee,
The mouse has married the bumble bee.'
Pipe, cat; dance, mouse;
We'll have a wedding at our good house.

Come dance a jig
To my granny's pig,
With a rowdy dowdy dowdy;
Come, dance a jig
To my granny's pig
And pussy-cat shall crowdy.

[31]

This nursery tale dates back first to Aesop's tales, then it was used in the medieval story of Reynard the Fox. Centuries later, Thomas and John Bewick used it for their book, *Select Fables*.

As a Cat and a Fox were talking politics together, in the middle of a forest, Reynard said, 'Let things turn out ever so bad, he did not care, for he had a thousand tricks for them yet, before they should hurt him; but pray,' says he, 'Mrs Puss, suppose there should be an invasion, what course do you design to take?' 'Nay,' says the Cat, 'I have but one shift for it, and if that won't do, I am undone.' 'I am sorry for you,' replies Reynard, 'with all my heart, and would gladly furnish you with one or two of mine, but indeed, neighbour, as times go, it is not good to trust; we must even be every one for himself, as the saying is, and so your humble servant.' These words were scarce out of his mouth, when they were alarmed by a pack of hounds that came upon them full cry. The Cat, by the help of her single shift, ran up a tree, and sat securely among the top branches; from whence she beheld Reynard who had not been able to get out of sight, overtaken with his thousand tricks, and torn in as many pieces by the dogs which had surrounded him.

Reflection.
A man that sets up for more cunning than the rest of his neighbours, is generally a silly fellow at the bottom... One good discreet expedient made use of upon an emergency, will do a man more real service, and make others think better of him, than to have passed all along for a shrewd crafty knave, and be bubbled at last.

Ann and Jane Taylor published *Original Poems for Infant Minds* in 1804 when they were respectively only twenty-two and nineteen-years old. Their best-known poem is *Twinkle, Twinkle, Little Star*. They must have been cat lovers, for many of their poems are about cats and all of them suggest kindness to felines. This one, *The Frolicsome Kitten*, has not just one moral but two!

> Dear kitten, do lie still, I say,
> I really want you to be quiet,
> Instead of scampering away,
> And always making such a riot.
>
> There only see! you've torn my frock,
> And poor Mamma must put a patch in,
> I'll give you a right earnest knock,
> And cure you of this trick of scratching.
>
> Nay, do not scold your little cat,
> She does not know what 'tis you're saying;
> And every time you give a pat,
> She thinks you mean it all for playing.
>
> But if poor pussy understood
> The lesson that you want to teach her,
> And did not choose to be so good,
> She'd be, indeed, a naughty creature.

[33]

The Taylor sisters believed that a child that was cruel to animals would grow up to be a person who is cruel to other people. Modern studies have shown that this is probably true: disturbed children who torture animals grow up to be adults who abuse other humans. Here is one of their poems on the subject – *The Cruel Boy and the Kittens.*

What! go to see kitten drowned,
On purpose in the yard!
I did not think there could be found
A little heart so hard.

Poor kittens! no more pretty play
With pussy's wagging tail:
Oh! I'd go far enough away
Before I'd see the pail.

Poor things! the little child that can
Be pleased to go and see,
Most likely, when he grows a man,
A cruel man will be.

And many a wicked thing he'll do,
Because his heart is bad:
A great deal worse than killing you,
Poor kittens, in the yard.

This nursery rhyme comes from a collection made by the poet Robert Graves. Some people believe that, though he did not admit it, he wrote it himself. In the War of the Roses two great families, that of York whose emblem was the white rose and that of Lancaster whose emblem was the red, contended for the throne of England.

The War of the Roses

Huff the talbot and our cat Tib
They took up sword and shield,
Tib for the red rose, Huff for the white,
To fight upon Bosworth Field.

Oh, it was dreary that night to bury
Those doughty warriors dead,
Under a white rose brave dog Huff,
And fierce Tib under a red.

Low lay Huff and long may he lie!
But our Tib took little harm:
He was up and away at dawn of day
With the rose-bush under his arm.

Victorian Alphabet Cats

In **A**dam's fall,
We sinned all.
Thy Life to mend,
This **B**ook attend.
The **C**at doth play,
And after slay.

D is for Dog,
Loyal, faithful and true.
I hope he gets married
To Pussy, don't you?

C stands for the Cats who live in your house,
They love milk and meat, but most a fat mouse.

Great **A**, little **a**,
Bouncing **B**;
The cat's in the cupboard
And she can't see me.

D'Arcy Wentworth Thompson was a Scottish teacher who wrote an early book of nonsense rhymes. *Nursery Nonsense*, published in 1864, had two delightful cat poems in it.

The Dear Little Cat

Who's that ringing at my door bell?
I'm a little pussy-cat and I'm not very well.
Then rub your little nose with a little mutton fat,
And that's the best thing for a sick pussy cat.

Very Poorly

Two cats sat on a garden wall,
For an hour or so together;
First they talked about nothing at all,
And then they talked of the weather.

The Owl and the Pussy-Cat

The Owl and the Pussy-Cat went to sea
In a beautiful pea-green boat;
They took some honey, and plenty of money
Wrapped up in a five-pound note.
The Owl looked up to the moon above,
And sang to a small guitar:
'O lovely Pussy! O Pussy, my love!
What a beautiful Pussy you are, – you are,
What a beautiful Pussy you are!'

Pussy said to the owl: 'You elegant fowl!
How charmingly sweet you sing!
O let us be married – too long we have tarried –
But what shall we do for a ring?'
They sailed away for a year and a day
To the land where the Bong-tree grows,
And there in a wood, a Piggy-wig stood
With a ring in the end of his nose, – his nose,
With a ring in the end of his nose.

[38]

Dear Pig, are you willing to sell for one shilling
Your ring?' Said the Piggy, 'I will.'
So they took it away, and were married next day
By the turkey who lives on the hill.
They dined upon mince and slices of quince,
Which they ate with a runcible spoon,
And hand in hand on the edge of the sand
They danced by the light of the moon, – the moon,
They danced by the light of the moon.

EDWARD LEAR

Among Edward Lear's papers when he died was a rough draft of a sequel to *The Owl and the Pussy-Cat*. Here are the first two verses.

Our mother was the Pussy-Cat, our father was the Owl,
And so we're partly little beasts and partly little fowl,
The brothers of our family have feathers and they hoot,
While all the sisters dress in fur and have long tails to boot.
We all believe that little mice,
For food are singularly nice.

Our mother died long years ago. She was a lovely cat,
Her tail was five feet long and grey with stripes, but
     what of that?
In Sila forest on the East of far Calabria's shore
She tumbled from a lofty tree – none ever saw her more.
Our owly father long was ill from sorrow and surprise,
But with the feathers of his tail he wiped his
     weeping eyes.
And in the hollow of a tree in Sila's inmost maze
We made a happy home and there we pass our
     obvious days.

CATS BY THE FIRESIDE

'A house without a cat, and a well-fed, well-petted, and properly revered cat, may be a perfect house, perhaps, but how can it prove its title?' wrote Mark Twain in *Pudd'nhead Wilson*. If a house is to be a home, it needs a cat.

Some, like the poet Robert Southey, go further and say that every home should have a kitten. 'A house is never perfectly furnished for enjoyment, unless there is a child in it rising three years old, and a kitten rising six weeks,' he wrote. 'Kitten is in the animal world what the rosebud is in the garden; the one the most beautiful of all young creatures, the other the loveliest of all opening flowers.'

Cats, it is true, are home-loving creatures belonging to places as well as people. Even cats that accompany their owners about the house and garden, will generally turn for home when their humans go for a walk. Early naturalists, failing to understand this territorial behaviour, condemned their failure to follow man.

'The nature of this beast is, to love the place of her breeding, neither will she tarry in any strange place, although carried far, being never willing to forsake the house, for the love of any man, and most contrary to the nature of a dog who will travaile abroad with his master,' wrote Edward Topsell, a Jacobean writer. 'They love fire and warm places, whereby it often falleth out that they often burn their coats.'

Yet how enlightening is this cat's sense of place. If we look round our home through the eyes of a cat, we see a different world. A cat knows that in the afternoon a shaft of sunlight will hit one of the armchairs, making it an ideal place for a post-lunch nap. It seeks out places on windowsills from which it operates a kind of feline neighbourhood watch on all that goes on outside. It finds odd places to nap – in the airing cupboard, on top of the piano, on a heap of newly dried washing, in a cardboard box, or inside a drawer.

Cats also help us humans to enjoy home comforts. They will sit purring on the hearth, their front paws tucked up underneath their bodies, their eyes reflecting the fire's glow. Curled up on our laps, their warm bodies and soothing purr helps us relax. Abraham Lincoln, the first United States President to keep a cat in the White House, found that his cat helped him wind down. 'When weariness set in,' wrote a biographer, 'he would stop thought, and get down and play with a little dog or kitten to recover.'

Into our artificial lives of ringing alarm clocks, crowded buses and trains, relentless traffic, and busy pavements, cats bring peace. There is no sight so calming as a happy cat asleep; no sound so comforting as a steady purr. As Konrad Lorenz put it, 'The purring cat is, for me, a symbol of the hearthside and the hidden security which it stands for.'

[42]

One of the best poems about a sleeping cat was written, rather surprisingly, by D.H. Lawrence. It conveys the animal's spiritual serenity.

Pax

All that matters is to be at one with the living God
To be a creature in the house of the God of Life.

Like a cat asleep on a chair,
At peace, in peace
And at one with the master of the house, with the mistress,
At home, at home in the house of the living,
Sleeping on the hearth, and yawning before the fire.

Sleeping on the hearth of the living world
Yawning at home before the fire of life
Feeling the presence of the living God
Like a great reassurance
A deep calm in the heart
A presence
As of the master sitting at the board
In his own and greater being,
In the house of life.

[43]

Leigh Hunt, the poet and critic, wrote an essay titled *The Cat by the Fire.* He described in detail the way a cat washes herself – and what a pleasure it is for human onlookers.

A blazing fire, a warm rug, candles lit and curtains drawn, the kettle on for tea… and finally the cat before you, attracting your attention, – it is a scene which everybody likes unless he has a morbid aversion to cats; which is not common.

Poor Pussy! She looks up at us… and symbolically gives a twist of a yawn and a lick to her whiskers. Now she proceeds to clean herself all over, having a just sense of the demands of her elegant person – beginning judiciously with her paws, and fetching amazing tongues at her hind-hips. Anon, she scratches her neck with a foot of rapid delight, leaning her head towards it, and shutting her eyes, half to accommodate the action of the skin and half to enjoy the luxury. She then rewards her paws with a few more touches; – look at the action of her head and neck, how pleasing it is, the ears pointed forward, and the neck gently arching to and fro. Finally she gives a sneeze, and another twist of mouth and whiskers, and then, curling her tail towards her front paws, settles herself on her hind quarters in an attitude of bland meditation… Cats at firesides live luxuriously, and are the picture of comfort.

The French dramatist and poet François Lemaître wrote a sonnet to his cat, translated here into blank verse.

Dearest cat, honoured guest of my old house,
Arch your supple, tingling back,
And curl upon my knee, to let me
Bathe my fingers in your warm fur.

Green eyes half closed mock me as they caress,
After a slow, luxurious shudder.
Gold flecked and drowsy, your eyes
Watch me ironic, yet benign.

Not for you, my philosophic old friend,
The blind devotion of a boisterous dog,
Yet my heart tells me that you love me still.

Your fleeting though understanding love
Satisfies me; and in you, serene thinker, I hail
Two subtler qualities – softness and doubt.

Milk for the Cat

When the tea is brought at five o'clock,
And all the neat curtains are drawn with care,
The little black cat with bright green eyes
Is suddenly purring there.

At first she pretends, having nothing to do,
She has come in merely to blink by the grate,
But, though tea may be late or the milk may be sour,
She is never late.

And presently her agate eyes
Take a soft large milky haze,
And her independent casual glance
Becomes a stiff hard gaze.

Then she stamps her claws or lifts her ears,
Or twists her tail and begins to stir,
Till suddenly all her lithe body becomes
One breathing trembling purr.

The children eat and wriggle and laugh;
The two old ladies stroke their silk:
But the cat is grown small and thin with desire,
Transformed to a creeping lust for milk.

The white saucer like some full moon descends
At last from the clouds of the table above;
She sighs and dreams and thrills and glows,
Transfigured with love.

She nestles over the shining rim,
Buries her chin in the creamy sea;
Her tail hangs loose; each drowsy paw
Is doubled under each bending knee.

A long dim ecstasy holds her life;
Her world is an infinite shapeless white,
Till her tongue has curled the last holy drop,
Then she sinks back into the night,

Draws and dips her body to heap
Her sleepy nerves in the great arm-chair,
Lies defeated and buried deep
Three or four hours unconscious there.

HAROLD MONRO

The poet William Cowper was a friend to all animals. He kept a spaniel, several cats, birds, and a tame hare. He lived quietly with his animals, a few close friends and his garden. His struggles against depression may have been the reason why he identified closely with suffering helpless animals. But he could also delight in animal joy too. Here is a letter he wrote to his cousin, Lady Hesketh, in 1787.

I have a kitten, my dear, the drollest of all creatures that ever wore a cat's skin. Her gambols are not to be described, and would be incredible if they could. She tumbles head over heels several times together, she lays her cheek to the ground and presents her rump at you with an air of most supreme disdain, from this posture she rises to dance on her hind feet, an exercise she performs with all the grace imaginable, and she closes those various exhibitions with a loud smack of her lips, which for want of greater propriety of expression we call spitting. But though all cats spit, no cat ever produced such a sound as she does. For point of size she is likely to be a kitten always, being extremely small of her age, but time I suppose, that spoils everything, will make her also a cat. You will see her I hope before that melancholy period shall arrive, for no wisdom that she may gain by experience, and reflect hereafter, will compensate the loss of her present hilarity. She is dressed in a tortoiseshell suit, and I know that you will like her.

This poem, *Comfort* by Walter De La Mare, is one of my favourites.

As I mused by the hearthside,
Puss said to me:
'There burns the Fire, man,
And here sit we.

Cats by the Fireside

'Four Walls around us
Against the cold air;
And the latchet drawn close
To the draughty Stair.

'A Roof o'er our heads
Star-proof, moon immune,
And a wind in the chimney
To wail us a tune.

'What Felicity' miaowed he,
'Where none may intrude;
Just Man and Beast – met
In this Solitude!

'Dear God, what security,
Comfort and bliss!
And to think, too, what ages
Have brought us to this!

'You in your sheep's-wool coat,
Buttons of bone,
And me in my fur-about
On the warm hearthstone.'

One of the earliest English books about cats had this splendid title – *The Book of Cats, a Chit-Chat Chronicle of Feline Facts and Fancies, Legendary, Lyrical, Medical, Mirthful and Miscellaneous*, written by Charles H. Ross and published in 1868.

We may learn some useful lessons from Cats, as indeed, from all animals… Cats may teach us patience and perseverance, and earnest concentration of mind on a desired object, as they watch for hours together by a mouse-hole, or in ambush for a bird… In their delicate walking amidst the fragile articles on a table or mantelpiece is illustrated the tact and discrimination by which we should thread rather than force our way; and, in pursuit of our own ends, avoid the injuring of others. In their noiseless tread and stealthy movements, we are reminded of the frequent importance of secrecy and caution prior to action, while their promptitude at the right moment, warns us, on the other hand, against the evils of irresolution and delay… As your Cat rubs her head against something you offer her, which she either does not fancy or does not want, she instructs you that there is a gracious mode of refusing a thing; and as she sits up like a bear, on her hind legs, to ask for something (which Cats will often do for a long time together), you may see the advantage of a winning and engaging way, as well when you are seeking a favour as when you think fit to decline one… A cat rolled up into a ball, or crouched with its paws folded underneath it, seems an emblem of repose and contentment. There is something soothing in the mere sight of it.

In *The Bachelor's Dream*, Thomas Hood muses on the pleasures of life with his cat and dog, as opposed to life with a wife.

My pipe is lit, my grog is mixed,
My curtains drawn and all is snug;
Old Puss is in her elbow-chair,
And Tray is sitting on the rug.
Last night I had a curious dream,
Miss Susan Bates was Mistress Mogg –
What d'ye think of that, my cat?
What d'ye think of that, my dog?

My Susan's taste was superfine,
As proved by bills that had no end –
I never had a decent coat –
I never had a coin to spend!
She forced me to resign my Club,
Lay down my pipe, retrench my grog –
What d'ye think of that, my cat?
What d'ye think of that, my dog?

Now was not that an awful dream
For one who single is and snug –
With Pussy in the elbow-chair
And Tray reposing on the rug? –
If I must totter down the hill,
'Tis safest done without a clog –
What d'ye think of that, my cat?
What d'ye think of that, my dog?

CATS ON THE TILES

The domestic cat, that sits purring so tamely in front of the fire, has a secret wild life outside. It will walk out into the garden to stalk its prey, seizing it with sharp claws before giving a death bite with its dagger-like front teeth. The instinct of the cat is to hunt – whether its prey is an expensive cat toy in the house or a defenceless little shrew in the garden.

This ability was highly valued in the past. Cats were natural pesticides, keeping down the numbers of mice and rats in farmyards, barns and mills. But, alas, it is not only mice that are caught. A study of what the cat brought home in an English village showed that they also caught sparrows, song thrushes, robins and blackbirds.

There is something devilish in the way a well-fed cat will play with a terrified mouse, batting it up in the air, pouncing again on it, then setting it free again so that the chase can go on. Like man, they will kill for sheer pleasure, not for hunger.

Above all, the cat can survive without man's help. It is truly independent. The cat, as the ethologist Konrad Lorenz puts it, 'remains an independent, wild, little panther'. It is a paradoxical pet – a tame animal with all the skills of a wild being.

In both town and country there are two cat populations – the plump pet moggies, fed to the brim with expensive cat food, and the wild or half-wild strays which live off the mice in the fields and barns or plunder the town's dustbins at night. Some cats move between these two worlds with ease and the angel in the home becomes the devil outside on the streets.

This way cats have the best of both worlds – regular meals and warm naps under the radiator inside, and the excitement of exploring the rooftops, hunting, and perhaps fighting outside. We often do not know much about the private lives of our own cats. From inside the house we hear the unearthly caterwauls of a mating ritual or mysterious spitting stand-offs for territory.

This wildness at the heart of a cat is a great attraction to the true cat lover. Animal lovers though we are, we may feel a pang of pride, when we see our cat proudly bringing home a large mouse or even, maybe, a rabbit. Perhaps the cat's hunter heart speaks to the savage instinct, that is still alive in women and men despite thousands of years of suppression.

Three or four generations ago, the cat's hunting instinct was taken for granted. Poets and writers saw it merely as part of its usefulness to man. But as civilisation imposes its petty rules and regulations on us all, it becomes a thing to marvel at.

Once the dog had all the best poems: now modern poetry celebrates the cat more often than the dog. For the cat is a hero for our times – an aristocat ignoring rules, a being which keeps its independence while showing affection, an irrepressible free spirit. In a crowded, regulated and increasingly bureau-cratic world, the cat retains a freedom we humans have lost.

The Conscience of a Cat

A dog will often steal a bone,
But conscience lets him not alone,
And by his tail his guilt is known.

But cats consider theft a game
And, howsoever you may blame,
Refuse the slightest sign of shame.

When food mysteriously goes,
The chances are that Pussy knows
More than she leads you to suppose.

And hence there is no need for you,
If Puss declines a meal or two,
To feel her pulse or make ado.

AUTHOR UNKNOWN

Nearly eight hundred years ago an English medieval Franciscan friar, called Bartholomew, published an encyclopaedia with the title, *The Property of Things*. It covered science, manners, medicine, geography and zoology. This description of a cat comes from a translation made in 1535.

The cat is a beast of uncertain hair and colour; for some cat is white, some red, some black, some spewed and speckled in the feet, and in the face and in the ears. He is a full lecherous beast in youth, swift, pliant and merry, and leapeth and reseth on everything that is to fore him: and is led by a straw and playeth therewith: and is a right heavy beast in age and full sleepy, and lieth slyly in wait for mice: and is more aware where they be by smell than by sight, and hunteth and reseth on them in privy places: and when he taketh a mouse, he playeth therewith, and eateth him after the play. In time of love is hardfighting for wives, and one scratcheth and rendeth the other grievously with biting and claws. And he maketh a ruthful noise and ghastful, when one proffereth to fight with another: and unneth is hurt when is is thrown down off a high place.

This poem, *Snow in the Suburbs*, has only two lines about a cat, but the image of the freezing cat being let in to the warm house stays in my mind. The poet Thomas Hardy loved all cats and his letters to his wife give news of all the household cats.

Every branch big with it,
Bent every twig with it;
Every fork like a white web-foot;
Every street and pavement mute:
Some flakes have lost their way, and grope back upward, when
Meeting those meandering down they turn and descend again.
The palings are glued together like a wall,
And there is no waft of wind with the fleecy fall.

A sparrow enters the tree,
Whereon immediately
A snow-lump thrice his own slight size
Descends on him and showers his head
    and eyes.
And overturns him,
And near inurns him,
And lights on a nether twig, when its brush
Starts off a volley of other lodging lumps
    with a rush.

The steps are a blanched slope,
Up which, with feeble hope,
A black cat comes, wide-eyed and thin:
And we take him in.

The ethologist Konrad Lorenz was one of the first modern scientists to study not just wild animals, but the domestic companions of man.

Only two animals have entered the human household otherwise than as prisoners and become domesticated by other means than those of enforced servitude: the dog and the cat... In the manner of their association with man, they are as different as the night from the day... There is no animal that, in the course of its century-old association with man, has altered so little as the cat. There is some truth in the assertion that the cat, with the exception of a few luxury breeds, such as Angoras, Persians and Siamese, is no domestic animal but a completely wild being. Maintaining its full independence it has taken up its abode in the houses and outhouses of man, for the simple reason that there are more mice there than elsewhere. The whole charm of the dog lies in the depth of the friendship and the strength of the spiritual ties with which he has bound himself to man, but the appeal of the cat lies in the very fact that she has formed no close bond with him, that she has the uncompromising independence of a tiger or a leopard while she is hunting in his stables and barns: that she still remains mysterious and remote when she is rubbing herself gently against the legs of her mistress or purring contentedly in front of the fire.

Minnaloushe belonged to Maud Gonne, the woman who inspired the love of William Butler Yeats. He immortalised him in *The Cat and the Moon.*

The cat went here and there
And the moon spun round like a top,
And the nearest kin of the moon,
The creeping cat, looked up.
Black Minnaloushe stared at the moon,
For, wander and wail as he would,
The pure cold light in the sky
Troubled his animal blood.
Minnaloushe runs in the grass
Lifting his delicate feet.
Do you dance, Minnaloushe, do you dance?
When two close kindred meet,
What better than call a dance?
Maybe the moon may learn,
Tired of that courtly fashion,
A new dance turn.
Minnaloushe creeps through the grass
From moonlit place to place,
The sacred moon overhead
Has taken a new phase.
Does Minnaloushe know that his pupils
Will pass from change to change,
And that from round to crescent,
From crescent to round they range?
Minnaloushe creeps through the grass
Alone, important and wise,
And lifts to the changing moon
His changing eyes.

In his journal, which was published after his death, Henry David Thoreau, the American poet, essayist and philosopher, noted the behaviour of his cats. I share his feeling of wonder that there can be such a 'society' or friendship between human and cat species.

28 September
As the lion is said to lie in a thicket or in tall reeds and grass by day, slumbering, and sally out at night, just so with the cat. She will ensconce herself for the day in the grass or weeds in some out-of-the-way nook near the house, and arouse herself toward night.

29 October
The cat comes stealthily creeping towards some prey amid the withered flowers in the garden, which being disturbed by my approach, she runs low toward it, with an unusual glare or superficial light in her eye, ignoring her oldest acquaintance, as wild as her remotest ancestor...

12 December
Wonderful, wonderful is our life, and that of our companions! That there should be such a thing as a brute animal, not human! that it should attain to a sort of our society with our race! Think of cats, for instance; they are neither Chinese nor Tartars, they neither go to school, nor read the Testament. Yet how near they come to doing so, how much they are like us who do.

The Cat of the House

I muse
Over the hearth with my 'minishing eyes
Until after
The last coal dies.
Every tunnel of the mouse,
Every channel of the cricket,
I have smelt.
I have felt
The secret shifting of the mouldered rafter,
And heard
Every bird in the thicket…
I, born of a race of strange things,
Of deserts, great temples, great kings,
In the hot sands where the nightingale never sings!
Old he-gods of ingle and hearth,
Young she-gods of fur and silk –
Not mud of the earth –
Are the things I dream of.

FORD MADOX FORD

Sometimes cats give children the love which parents cannot. Hector Hugh Monro, who wrote under the pseudonym of 'Saki', was brought up in such a home. As a result, he loved and understood cats.

The cat is domestic only as far as suits its own ends; it will not be kennelled or harnessed nor suffer any dictation as to its goings out or comings in. Long contact with the human race has developed in it the art of diplomacy, and no Roman Cardinal of medieval days knew better how to ingratiate himself with his surroundings than a cat with a saucer of cream on its mental horizon. But the social smoothness, the purring innocence, the softness of the velvet paw may be laid aside at a moment's notice, and the sinuous feline may disappear, in deliberate aloofness, to a world of roofs and chimney-stacks, where the human element is distanced and disregarded. Or the innate savage spirit that helped its survival in the bygone days of tooth and claw may be summoned forth from beneath the sleek exterior, and the torture instinct (common alone to human and feline) may find free play in the death throes of some luckless bird or rodent. It is, indeed, no small triumph to have combined the untrammelled liberty of primeval savagery with the luxury which only a highly-developed civilisation can command; to be lapped in the soft stuffs that commerce has gathered from the far ends of the world; to bask in the warmth that labour and industry have dragged from the bowels of the earth; to banquet on the dainties that wealth has bespoken for its table, and withal to be a free son of nature, a mighty hunter, a spiller of life-blood. This is the victory of the cat.

However pampered, a cat will still hunt. Taken to the countryside, even town cats take to mousing with the same clumsy enthusiasm that is shown by plump businessmen who go shooting at weekends. Pleasure, not hunger, is the motive. The fourteenth-century poet Geoffrey Chaucer has some lines on the cat's compulsion to hunt.

> But God it woot, there may no man embrace
> As to distrain a thing which that nature
> Hath naturally set in a creature…
> Let take a cat and foster him well with milk
> And tender flesh and make his couch of silk,
> And let him seen a mouse go by the wall,
> Anon he waveth milk and flesh and all,
> And every dainty that is in that house,
> Such appetite he hath to eat a mouse.

An Appeal to Cats in the Business of Love

Ye cats that at midnight spit love at each other,
Who best feel the pangs of a passionate lover,
I appeal to your scratches and your tattered fur,
If the business of love be no more than to purr.
Old Lady Grimalkin with her gooseberry eyes,
Knew something when a kitten, for why she was wise;
You find by experience, the love-fit's soon o'er,
Puss! Puss! lasts not long, but turns to *Cat-whore!*
    Men ride many miles,
    Cats tread many tiles,
    Both hazard their necks in the fray;
    Only cats, when they fall
    From a house or a wall,
    Keep their feet, mount their tails, and away!

THOMAS FLATMAN

Cats often choose their owners. Street cats, and sometimes cats who already have a home but just fancy a change, are also very good at finding new homes. In one of my favourite passages, Jerome K. Jerome reveals how a cat changed homes whenever it suited her. This is the cat's advice on how to manipulate humans.

I tell you how easy it is to be 'taken in'. Fix on your house, and mew piteously at the back door. When it is opened, run in and rub yourself against the first leg you come across. Rub hard, and look up confidingly. Nothing gets round human beings, I have noticed, quicker than confidence. They don't get much of it, and it pleases them. Always be confiding. At the same time, be prepared for emergencies. If you are still doubtful as to your reception, try and get yourself slightly wet. Why people should prefer a wet cat to a dry one I have never been able to understand, but that a wet cat is practically sure of being taken in and gushed over, while a dry cat is liable to have the garden hose turned upon it, is an undoubted fact. Also, if you can possibly manage it, and if it is offered to you, eat a bit of dried bread. The Human Race is always stirred to its deepest depths by the sight of a cat eating a bit of dry bread.

CATS – CELEBRATED AND ECCENTRIC

It is impossible to imagine a team of cats, a regiment of cats, or even a collection of cats, each working together. No wonder, therefore, that there is no common collective word to describe an assemblage of cats. Other animals live in herds, packs, or flocks. Not cats.

The cat walks by itself, even when in the company of other cats. Each cat is an individual personality. As the poet Robert Southey put it: 'Cats have characters – and for the benefit of philosophy, as well as felisophy, this truth ought to be generally known.'

In literature, one of the first individual cats that comes to our attention is Pangur Ban, the white cat that belonged to a scholar, probably a monk. He was the subject of a poem in Gaelic, which was found in the Irish monastery of St Paul. The manuscript dates back to the ninth century AD. It is probably the first loving poem about an individual cat not just in British, but in any literature.

Pangur Ban is quite a conventional cat in his activities but some cats make their mark by extraordinary behaviour. A century ago, there was a fishing cat living at Devil's Point, one of the defence works in the naval port of Plymouth. Every day she dived off the rocky shore into the sea, caught a fish, and carried it to the naval guard room to show off her prize.

Another famous cat was the hero-mog of Stalingrad during the last world war. While the Russian city was under terrible siege by the Germans, Mourka would carry messages from a group of Russian scouts to a house across the street. Admittedly the company kitchen was situated in the house, to which he bore dispatches, and as a *Times* leader in 1943 put it: 'some, with the cavilling peculiar to vulgar minds, will see in this more than a coincidence.'

Occasionally, if it pleases them, cats behave as faithfully as dogs and cats have proved their fidelity unto death. In *Friends in Fur*, a Victorian writer, W. Gordon Stables, tells the story of an old fiddler who lived alone but for his cat. After his death, his cat followed his body to the grave. 'She never left that churchyard living. For three days she sat on the grave... On a cold sleety morning in November she was found stretched on the grave – in a hole she had scraped – dead.'

Sometimes cats make friends with other species. The poet John Clare had a tame house sparrow that grew to be great friends with his cat. She adopted it after the poet took away her kittens, and she would bring mice for it and chirrup to it.

What surprises me is the adaptability of cats. Though they may refuse to be trained by human beings, cats can (if they so choose) adapt to quite unusual circumstances. In the past cats have been used as hunting animals, gardening assistants, and even in one case as military weapons. Sometimes this is simply the result of feline eccentricity. Some of the cats in this chapter were unusual personalities who chose the path less trodden. Some are perhaps fictional rather than actual cats. But let us nonetheless praise famous or remarkable cats.

One of the early English cat authors was Lady Julia Chance, in 1898. She was a go-ahead lady, keen on cycling. So was her cat, William.

Last year I took a little cat with me on a bicycle tour. It sat in a basket on the handle bars, and appeared to enjoy everything except 'coasting'. Like Gunga Din it 'didn't seem to know the use of fear' and its composure was never ruffled. It went down the Wye in a boat, it travelled by rail and in carts or buses. It went through its ablutions on the crowded platform of Bristol Station with the utmost nonchalance. It went for long country walks, following like a dog, and jumping carefully over the puddles, and delicately avoiding wet places. If a cart came along it would spring into the bushes at the side of the road and sit like Brer Rabbit in the briar patch, with just its head sticking out.

A very pleasure feature of William's tour was the warm welcome he received from everyone whose hospitality he enjoyed. Rather to my surprise the innkeepers at the places where we stopped, far from objecting to such a strange travelling companion, without exception, made quite a fuss about him, and petted and admired him to an extent which should have turned his head.

William is now too heavy to go out cycling but he still goes for walks when we can take him with us without risk of meeting strange dogs. His extreme fearlessness increases the danger as I very much doubt if he would realise that there could be any necessity for defending himself.

The French have been ahead of us in the loving description of their feline friends. The novelist Theophile Gautier told the story of his many cats in *A Domestic Menagerie*. Eponine was one of the most striking in her gentility and charm.

> Eponine attached herself particularly to me… She comes running up when she hears the front door bell, receives the visitors, conducts them to the drawing room, talks to them – yes, talks to them – with little chirruping sounds, that do not in the least resemble the language cats use in talking to their own kind, but which simulate the articulate speech of man… Then when I come in she discreetly retires to an armchair or a corner of the piano, like a well bred animal who knows what is correct in good society. Pretty little Eponine gave so many proofs of intelligence, good disposition and sociability, that by common consent she was raised to the dignity of a *person*… This dignity conferred on her the privilege of eating at table like a person instead of out of a saucer in the corner of the room like an animal.
>
> So Eponine had a chair next to me at breakfast and dinner, but on account of her small size she was allowed to rest her two front paws on the edge of the table. Her place was laid without spoon or fork, but she had her glass. She went right through the dinner dish by dish, from soup to dessert, waiting for her turn to be helped, and behaving with such propriety and nice manners as one would like to see in many children. She made her appearance at the first sound of the bell, and on going into the dining room one found her already in her place, sitting up in her chair with her paws resting on the edge of the tablecloth, and seeming to offer you her little face to kiss, like a well-brought-up little girl who is affectionately polite towards her parents and elders.
>
> As one finds flaws in diamonds, spots on the sun, and shadows on perfection itself, so Eponine, it must be confessed, had a passion

for fish… She became nearly frantic over fish, and, like a child who is filled with the expectation of dessert, she sometimes rebelled at her soup when she knew (from previous investigations in the kitchen) that fish was coming. When this happened she was not helped, and I would say to her coldly: 'Mademoiselle, a person who is not hungry for soup cannot be hungry for fish,' and the dish would be pitilessly carried away from under her nose. Convinced that matters were serious, greedy Eponine would swallow her soup in all haste, down to the last drop, polishing off the last crumb of bread or bit of macaroni, and would then turn round and look at me with pride, like someone who has conscientiously done his duty. She was then given her portion, which she consumed with great satisfaction…

A Music Hall Song

A downy cove is our old tom cat,
Just turned thirty years old;
He eateth the lean, and leaveth the fat,
And won't touch his meals when too cold.
His food must be crumbled, and not decayed,
To pleasure his dainty whim,
But a turkey bone from the kitchen-maid
Is a very good meal for him.

Chorus:
Creeping over the tiles pit pat,
A downy cove is the old tom cat.

Whole joints have fled, and their bones decayed,
And dishes have broken been,
But old tom still follows the kitchen-maid,
And slyly licks up the cream.
Now, old tom cat, in his lonely days,
Shall joyously think of the past,
And a big leg of mutton, that never was touched,
Shall be food for our Tommy at last.

Fast creepeth he, though he hath no wings,
And a sly old dodger is he,
As under the garret window he sings –
Ain't you coming out tonight, love, to me?
Then slyly he creepeth the gutters all round,
And his old tail he joyously waves,
As his lady love from a garret he spies,
And he sings his amorous staves.

Sometimes cat enthusiasts go too far in their felophilia. Dr Gordon Stables was a Victorian pets writer and his book, *Cats*, includes this unlikely story about feline gymnasts.

A very pretty and effective exercise for a cat is hoop-leaping. It costs little trouble to teach and every cat will learn it. For this you must be provided with a little switch, not to hit the cat, but merely to make a noise in the air. Pronounce the word hoop each time you hold the article in front of her, and she will soon learn to go through it in whatever position you hold it. Or you may have a series of hoops, at different elevations, placed in the garden a few yards apart; or, better still, hung from the couples of a barn or grain-loft. On these last a young and healthy cat soon becomes quite a wonderful performer; and, if you wish her to be still more highly educated in the hoop business, you can dip your hoop in methylated spirits of wine and set fire to it; she will go through just the same. Or cover the hoop with thin tissue paper and teach her to go through it. At first the paper must be oiled so as to be nearly transparent. A friend of mine, coming home at twelve o'clock, heard an awful noise and rattling in an out-house which he had fitted up as a cat gymnasium. On going in with a light he was surprised to find two full grown kittens performing – they had been giving a dark seance on their own account.

Unlike dogs, cats have resisted most attempts to involve them in human warfare. They refused to obey orders during an American attempt to use them as night guides for soldiers during the Vietnam war. The cats simply led off in pursuit of mice, or stalked the dangling straps of the soldier in front!

The only known successful deployment of cats in warfare occurred in the ancient world under the Persian ruler Cambyses in 525 BC. This was put on record by a retired soldier, Polyaenus the Macedonian, in a book called *Stratagems of War*, written seven hundred years later.

> When Cambyses invested Pelusium, as being the entrance to Egypt, the Egyptians with great resolution defended it, advancing formidable machines against the besiegers and from the catapults throwing darts, stones and fire. Cambyses ranged before his front line dogs, sheep, cats, ibises, and whatever animals the Egyptians hold sacred. The fear of hurting the animals, which they regard with veneration, instantly checked their operations. Cambyses took Pelusium and thus opened himself a passage into Egypt.

A rum feline story comes from the humorous writer Jerome K. Jerome. I include it because it makes me laugh, even if it isn't true.

> My grandmother's cat, after living a blameless life for upwards of eleven years, took to drink in her old age and was run over while in a state of intoxication (oh, the justice of it!) by a brewer's dray...
>
> A leaky beer-tap was the cause of her downfall. A saucer used to be placed underneath to catch the drippings. One day the cat, coming in thirsty and finding nothing else to drink, lapped up a little, liked it, and lapped a little more, went away for half an hour, and came back and finished the saucerful – then sat down beside it and waited for it to fill up again.

From that day till the hour she died, I don't think that cat was ever once sober. Her days she passed in a drunken stupor before the kitchen fire. Her nights she spent in the beer cellar.

My grandmother, shocked and grieved beyond expression, gave up her beer barrel and adopted bottles. The cat, thus condemned to enforced abstinence, meandered about the house for a day and half in a disconsolate, quarrelsome mood. Then she disappeared, returning at eleven o'clock as tight as a drum.

Where she went, and how she managed to procure the drink, we never discovered; but the same programme was repeated every day. Some time during the morning she would contrive to elude our vigilance and escape; and late every evening she would come reeling home across the fields in a condition that I will not sully my pen by attempting to describe.

It was on a Saturday night that she met the sad end to which I have before alluded. She must have been very drunk, for the man told us that, because of the darkness and because his horses were tired, he was proceeding at little more than a snail's pace.

Cats sometimes chum up with racehorses. The Godolphin Arabian was one of the great founders of the modern thoroughbred. Stubbs painted this famous racing sire, with his friend the cat. Here is an early account of the friendship, written by John Lawrence in *The History of Delineation of the Horse*, published in 1809.

The Arabian served for the remainder of his life in the same stud, producing a yearly succession of prodigies of the species. He died in 1753, in his twenty-ninth year, and his remains were desposited in a covered passage leading to the stable, a flat and thankless stone, bare of any inscription, being placed over him. The mutual attachment of animals of a different genus, when placed in a state of society, has often been remarked. Thus there was a reciprocal affection, of many years standing, between the Godolphin Arabian and a black cat, and a portrait of the cat was taken with that of the horse. Poor puss would not long survive her friend. She placed herself, seemingly in a mournful attitude, upon his dead carcase, where she remained fixed until it was removed from the building, then followed it to the place of burial under the gateway near the running stable, sat upon it whilst it continued above ground, and afterwards crawled slowly and reluctantly away, and was never seen again, until her dead body was found in the hayloft.

The earliest English reference to gardening cats comes in a medieval translation of a Latin book, *De Rerum Naturae*. It recommends cats to kill moles – 'for moldywarpes cattes is to keep, to ligge in wayte to touch hem with her cle.' Alas, no cat of mine has deterred moles. More effective gardening cats occur in the *Transactions of the Horticultural Society*, 1832.

I beg leave to communicate to the Society an easy method of preserving fruit trees and gardens from the depredation of birds, as adopted by my friend, Robert Brooke, Esq... He has four or five Cats, each with a collar, a light chain and swivel, about a yard long with a large iron ring at the end; as soon as gooseberries, currants and raspberries begin to ripen, a small stake is driven into the ground or bed, near the trees to be protected, leaving about a yard and a half of the stake above ground; the ring is slipped over the head of the stake, and the cat thus tethered in the sight of trees, no birds will approach them. Cherry trees and wall fruit trees are protected in the same manner as they successively ripen; each cat, by way of a shed, has one of the largest sized flower pots laid on its side, within reach of its chain, with a little hay or straw in bad weather, and her food and water placed near her.

Cat's Meat

You, who've rejected the pick of the dish
And flatly refuse to be stirred
By the mention of meat, if you know there is fish,
Or of fish, if you know there is bird,
Who insist on your sole being *à la bonne femme*,
And your chicken direct from the breast,
Who will only touch trout that has recently come
From the shadowy shoals of the Test,
You who drink nothing that isn't Grade A
And would turn up your nose at a mouse,
Whom I've actually seen moving coldly away
From an underhung portion of grouse,
You who will listlessly trifle and toy
With a dream of a cod kedgeree,
Are eating with every appearance of joy
A very decayed bumble bee.

AUTHOR UNKNOWN

The story of another brave and resourceful cat was immortalised in an inscription in a City of London church. Alas, it has now been removed.

On Monday, 9 September, 1940, she endured horrors and perils beyond the power of words to tell.

Shielding her kitten in a sort of recess in the house (a spot she selected only three days before the tragedies occurred), she sat the whole frightful night of bombing and fire, guarding her little kitten.

The roofs and masonry exploded, the whole house blazed, four floors fell through in front of her. Fire and ruin all around her.

Yet she stayed calm and steadfast and waited for help.

We rescued her in the early morning while the place was still burning, and by the mercy of Almighty God she and her kitten were not only saved, but unhurt.

Pangur Ban

Pangur, my white cat, and I,
We each a different skill apply;
His art is all in hunting mice,
Mine is in thought, deep and precise.

My greatest joy is just to sit
And con my page with subtle wit;
While Pangur Ban will frisk and play
Nor envy me my quieter way.

We are companions, never bored
In our small house, in true accord
We test our faculties, and find
Some occupation for the mind.

He, by his arts, can trap and kill
A hapless mouse with perfect skill.
And I, after much careful gleaning
Can bring to light a hidden meaning.

His eye, as keen as any sword,
Is focused on the skirting board;
While I direct my milder looks
Upon the knowledge in my books.

When he pursues a mouse with speed,
Pangur rejoices in the deed;
I exult when in the brain
Some knotty point at last comes plain.

Though we are always thus together,
We neither one obstruct the other;
Pangur and I pursue alone
Two separate arts, to each his own.

His curious work is his delight,
Which he rehearses day and night;
And daily I bring clarity
Where there had been obscurity.

Trans. GERARD BENSON

CATS AND MORTALITY

The beauty of cats, like the beauty of the natural world, is transient. They change from playful kittens into sleek cats, then slowly decline through the years. Yet even in arthritic old age, a gracefulness remains to them. Then comes that last fateful visit to the vet: we go back to an empty house and to mourning. Time diminishes the pain but the loss of a living personality is never quite healed.

Ancient Egyptians formally mourned their cats. 'Dwellers in a house where a cat has died a natural death shave their eyebrows,' reported the early historian Herodotus in the fourth century BC. 'Dead cats are taken away into sacred buildings, where they are embalmed and buried, in the town of Bubastis.' Thousands of years later archeologists still find their little mummies.

We moderns, who dote on our cats, are less fortunate than the Egyptians. There is little recognition that the loss of a cat will leave its human friend hurt and grieving. For most of us there is no ceremony of death – neither funeral prayers nor burial nor the attendance of friends. Our hearts have to break without acknowledgement.

Some of those who love cats have risked the jeers and made their loss public. The son-in-law of the Italian poet Petrarch had the poet's cat killed and embalmed after he had died, so that they could be together in death. In

1741, an Italian writer, Domenico Balestrieri, published the first anthology of cat poems written by himself and his friends after the death of his cat, with the title *Labrime in Morto di un Gatto* or *Tears on the Death of a Cat*.

Yet, with the exception of a lovely poem written by the nature poet John Clare, there are few great epitaphs for cats. John Keats wrote a sensitive poem about the old age of a cat. There are two poems about the death of cats by Thomas Hardy. Most poets, however, remained silent.

True animal lovers know what a blow it is to lose a feline friend. In 1862, the Victorian vicar and poet Robert Stephen Hawker wrote a series of comforting letters to a young woman who had lost her cat. 'I do not hesitate to call the loss of your pet a trouble, because to me there could be none worse,' he told her.

He believed, as I try to, that animals like humans survive into a life after death. 'They were created before Adam... They had a right in Paradise. They were gathered with the eight souls into the ark... When Jesus was born, it was in the presence of animals. The ox knew his Owner in the cave of Bethlehem, and the ass his Master's crib. In the wilderness the Son of Man was among the beasts of the wild. An ass knew her rider when he rode into Jerusalem royally... Who can read all this and doubt but that animals will roam and feed in the New Earth, wherein righteousness will dwell?'

A New Year's theme I strike upon my lyre for you.

The Roman Gravemounds

By Rome's dim relics there walks a man,
Eyes bent; and he carries a basket and spade;
I guess what impels him to scrape and scan;
Yea, his dreams of that Empire long decayed.

'Vast was Rome,' he must muse, 'in the world's regard,
Vast it looms there still, vast it ever will be',
And he stoops as to dig and unmine some shard
Left there by those who are held in such memory.

But no; in his basket, see, he has brought
A little white furred thing, stiff of limb,
Whose life never won from the world a thought;
It is this, and not Rome, that is moving him.

And to make it a grave he has come to the spot,
And he delves in the ancient dead's long home;
Their fames, their achievements the man knows not;
The furred thing is all to him – nothing Rome!

'Here say you that Caesar's warriors lie? -
But my little white cat was my only friend!
Could she but live, might the record die
Of Caesar, his legions, his arms, his end!'

THOMAS HARDY

A touching poem of mourning for his cat was written by John Clare. Here are some of its verses. A great poet, Clare was a farm worker at the beginning of the nineteenth century. In this poem he wrote without punctuation and spelled words as they sounded. It is called *Sorrows for a Favourite Tabby Cat who Left This Scene of Troubles Friday Night Nov. 26 1819.*

Ah pity, thines a tender heart
Thy sigh soon heaves thy tears will start
And thou has gen the muse her part
    Salt tears to shed
To mourn and sigh wi sorrows smart
    For pussey dead.

Ah mourning memory neath thy pall
Thou utterst many a piercing call
Pickling in vinegars sour gall
 Ways that are fled
The ways the feats the tricks and all
 Of pussey dead.

Thou tellst of all the gamsome plays
That markt her happy kitten days
– Ah I did love her funney ways
 On the sand floor
But now sad sorrow dampts my lays
 Pusseys no more

Thou paints her flirting round and round
As she was wont wi things she'd found
Chasing the spider oer the ground
 Straws pushing on
Thou paints em on a bosom wound
 Poor pusseys gone

And now poor puss thoust lost thy breath
And desent laid the moulds beneath
As ere a cat coud wish in death
 For their last bed
This to thy memory I bequeath
 Poor pussey dead

JOHN CLARE

The poet Robert Southey was one of those cat lovers who give their pets long and fanciful names. Some people see this as merely whimsical: I think it is a sign of love, like the absurd names that human lovers bestow on each other. Here is Southey writing to Grosvenor Bedford in May 1833 about the death of one of his favourites.

My dear G.

Alas, Grosvenor, this day poor old Rumpel was found dead, after as long and happy a life as cat could wish for, if cats form wishes on that subject.

His full titles were:-

The Most Noble the Archduke Rumpelstiltzchen, Marquis Macbum, Earl Tomlemagne, Baron Raticide, Waowhler, and Skaratch...

As we have no catacombs here, he is to be decently interred in the orchard, and cat-mint planted on his grave. Poor creature, it is well that he has thus come to his end after he had become an object of pity. I believe we are each and all, servants included, more sorry for his loss, or rather more affected by it, than anyone of us would like to confess.

Gerard Benson, the author of this poem, has always had cats. Grace was a very pale yellowish tabby, 'a pathological killer with the charm of a lap sitter'. With children she was patient and affectionate.

Grace, Our Tabby-Blonde

Grace, our tabby-blonde, whose plump 'murraoo!'
Conveyed such canny nuances of meaning,
    Has left us now.
Of late beside the fire she'd socialize,
Stretching her claws, or, indolently preening,
    Blink her slow eyes.

Time was, her style of manners was less nice,
When tribute from the garden she would fetch
    Of headless mice
Or ravaged finch. Agent she was for Death,
Who now, without remorse, ungrateful wretch,
    Has stopped her breath.

If heaven includes the reunion of those who have loved each other on earth, then my heaven will have to include Moppet, Fat Ada, and Bimbo, all my cats. Yet occasionally I have doubts about the true extent of feline virtue. Evelyn Underhill, the poet and religious writer, clearly shared in my hopes, and perhaps in my doubts too.

> Of course, I agree that animals too are involved in the Fall and await redemption and transfiguration. (Do you remember Luther looking up from Romans viii, 21 and saying to his dog, 'Thou too shalt have a little golden tail'?) And man is no doubt offered the chance of being the mediator of that redemption. But not by taming surely. Rather by loving and reverencing the creatures enough to leave them free. When my cat goes off on her own occasions I'm sure she goes with God – but I do not feel so sure of her theological position when she is sitting on the best chair before the drawing-room fire.

The poet John Keats deserves a place in this anthology if only because he once thrashed a man 'about cruelty to a cat'. A friend reported that he had 'had an encounter with a fellow who was tormenting a kitten, or puppy, and who was big enough to have eaten him: that they fought for nearly an hour; and that his opponent was led home'. A year earlier he had written this poem, *On Mrs Reynolds's Cat*.

Cat! who hast pass'd thy grand climacteric,
How many mice and rats hast in thy days
Destroy'd? – How many titbits stolen? Gaze
With those bright languid segments green,
    and prick
Those velvet ears – but pr'ythee do not
    stick
Thy latent talons in me – and upraise
Thy gentle mew – and tell me all thy
    frays
Of fish and mice, and rats and tender
    chick.
Nay, look not down, nor lick thy dainty
    wrists –
For all the wheezy asthma, – and for all
Thy tail's tip is nick'd off – and though the
    fists
Of many a maid have given thee many a maul,
Still is that fur as soft as when the lists
In youth thou enter'dst on glass-bottled wall.

It was in 1880 that the American writer Charles Dudley Warner added a postscript to his book, *My Summer in a Garden*. It was a memoir of his cat, Calvin. He added, 'in the hope that the record of an exemplary life in an humble sphere may be of some service to the world'.

As I look back upon it, Calvin's life seems to me a fortunate one, for it was natural and unforced. He ate when he was hungry, slept when he was sleepy, and enjoyed existence to the very tips of his toes and the end of his expressive and slow-moving tail. He delighted to roam about the garden and stroll among the trees, and to lie on the green grass and luxuriate in all the sweet influences of summer. You could never accuse him of idleness, and yet he knew the secret of repose. The poet who wrote so prettily of him that his little life was rounded with a sleep understated his felicity; it was rounded with a good many. His conscience never seemed to interfere with his slumbers. In fact, he had good habits and a contented mind. I can see him now walk in at the study door, sit down by my chair, bring his tail artistically about his feet, and look up at me with unspeakable happiness in his handsome face…

His departure was as quiet as his advent was mysterious. I only know that he appeared to us in this world in his perfect stature and beauty, and that after a time like Lohengrin, he withdrew. In his illness there was nothing more to be regretted than in all his blameless life... It came on gradually, in a kind of listlessness and want of appetite...He sat or lay day after day almost motionless... His favourite place was on the brightest spot of a Smyrna rug by the conservatory, where the sunlight fell and he could hear the fountain play. If we went to him and exhibited our interest in his condition, he always purred in recognition of our sympathy. And when I spoke his name, he looked up with an expression that said, 'I understand it, old fellow, but it's no use.' He was to all who came to visit him a model of calmness and patience in affliction...

One sunny morning he rose from his rug, went into the conservatory (he was very thin then), walked around it deliberately, looking at all the plants he knew, and then went to the bay-window in the dining room, and stood a long time looking out upon the little field, now brown and sere, and toward the garden, where perhaps the happiest hours of his life had been spent. It was a last look. He turned and walked away, laid himself down upon the bright spot in the rug, and quietly died.

Last Words to a Dumb Friend

Pet was never mourned as you,
Purrer of the spotless hue,
Plumy tail, and wistful gaze
While you humoured our queer ways,
Or outshrilled your morning call
Up the stairs and through the hall -
Foot suspended in its fall -
While, expectant, you would stand
Arched, to meet the stroking hand;
Till your way you chose to wend
Yonder to your tragic end.

Never another pet for me!
Let your place all vacant be;
Better blankness day by day
Than companion torn away.
Better bid his memory fade,
Better blot each mark he made,
Selfishly escape distress
By contrived forgetfulness,
Than preserve his prints to make
Every morn and eve an ache.

From the chair whereon he sat
Sweep his fur, nor wince thereat;
Rake his little pathways out
Mid the bushes round about;
Smooth away his talons' mark
From the claw-worn pine-tree bark,
Where he climbed as dusk enbrowned
Waiting us who loitered round.

Strange it is this speechless
    thing,
Subject to our mastering,
Subject for his life and food
To our gift, and time, and mood;
Timid pensioner of us Powers,
His existence ruled by ours,
Should - by crossing at a breath
Into safe and shielded death,
By the merely taking hence
Of his insignificance -
Loom as largened to the sense,
Shape as part, above man's will,
Of the Imperturbable…

Housemate, I can think you still
Bounding to the window-sill,
Over which I vaguely see
Your small mound beneath the tree,
Showing in the autumn shade
That you moulder where you played.

THOMAS HARDY

Acknowledgements

For permission to reproduce copyright material in this book, the author and publisher gratefully acknowledge the following:

Jess McAree, c/o Celia Haddon, for the translations of 'Happiness' by Hippolyte Taine and François Lemaître's sonnet to his cat; extract from Sir Edward Strachey Bart's introduction to *Nonsense Songs of Edward Lear* by permission of Frederick Warne; 'Pax' from *The Complete Poems of D.H. Lawrence* collected and edited by Vivian de Sola Pinto and F. Warren Roberts. Copyright © 1946, 1971 by Angelo Ravagli and C.M. Weekley, executors of the estate of Frieda Lawrence Ravagli. Reprinted by permission of the publisher, Viking Penguin, a division of Penguin Books USA Inc.; 'Comfort' by Walter de la Mare reprinted by permission of The Literary Trustees of Walter de la Mare and The Society of Authors as their representative; extract from *Man Meets Dogs* by Konrad Lorenz reprinted by permission of Methuen & Co. and the Joan Daves Agency; 'The Cat and the Moon' by W.B. Yeats reprinted with permission of Macmillan Publishing Company from *The Poems of W.B. Yeats: A New Edition*, edited by Richard J. Finneran. Copyright © 1919 by Macmillan Publishing Company, renewed 1947 by Bertha Georgie Yeats; Gerard Benson for permission to reprint 'Grace Our Tabby-Blonde' and his translation of 'Pangur Ban' (entitled in his translation 'The Scholar's Cat'). Gerard Benson may be contacted at 46 Ashwell Road, Manningham, Bradford 8, West Yorks, BD8 9DU; 'Sorrows for a Favourite Tabby Cat who Left This Scene of Troubles Friday Night. Nov. 28 1819' by John Clare from *The Early Poems of John Clare 1804–1822 Volume I*, © Eric Robinson 1989, reproduced by permission of Curtis Brown Ltd, London; 'The Cat of the House' by Ford Maddox Ford reprinted by permission of Janice Biala .

Picture Credits

Playing with the Kitten by Robert Collinson, the Christopher Wood Gallery, London/The Bridgeman Art Library; *Playmates* by William Henry Knight, Phillips the International Fine Art Auctioneers/The Bridgeman Art Library; *First Steps* by Carlton Alfred Smith, Towner Art Gallery, Eastbourne/The Bridgeman Art Library; *Reluctant Playmate* by Horatio Henry Couldery, Bonhams/The Bridgeman Art Library; *Mischievous Kittens* by Charles van den Eycken, by courtesy of Fine Art Photos; *A Cat in the Window of a Cottage* by Ralph Hedley, Laing Art Gallery, Newcastle-upon-Tyne/The Bridgeman Art Library.

Whilst every attempt has been made to trace the copyright holders, this has not always been possible. Any omissions will be rectified in future reprints